Table of Contents

How To Hear God's Voice

Eight Practical Steps To Help You Hear From God

By Tim Bader

We all struggle to hear God's voice, from time to time.
Discover eight simple ways to make it easier.

Introduction

We all struggle to hear God's voice, from time to time. Discover eight simple ways to make it easier.

Welcome to *How To Hear God's Voice: Eight practical steps to help you hear from God.* In these pages you'll find practical hints and tips to help you hear from God.

Whether you've known the Lord for a long time or have become a Christian only recently, my hope is that through this book you will find new opportunities to get close to God and have a deeper relationship with Him.

Who This Book Is For

How To Hear God's Voice is for anyone who wants to listen to God and understand more clearly what the Lord is saying to them.

If:

• you are seeking God's will for your life, perhaps for the first time,
• you have a gift of prophecy and are learning your skills, or
• you are sure of your prophetic gifting, but want to hear God in a deeper way,

…then this book is for you!

If you are in the third group (are sure of your prophetic gift) you may just want to quickly check the next section How To Use This Book and then jump straight from there to the tips in Part 2 .

Don't worry though, wherever you are in your Christian life, this book aims to help you get closer to God and hear him better.

How To Use This Book

How To Hear God's Voice is written in two parts:

Part 1, *Grappling With God* discusses why we need to have an encounter with God in order to hear him, and some of the issues we may face as we try to do that.

Part 2, *Hearing God*, goes through the "8 practical steps" that form the main substance of the book. I'll outline the steps you can take to place yourself in a position where you can hear God's voice. While I have tried to make things as practical as possible, hearing God is about relationship with him, first and foremost.

If you're building your relationship with the Lord, then I am confident you will learn how to hear him better. Of course, relationships take time, so developing your spiritual ears is not going to happen overnight. However, taking the practical steps outlined here can help to accelerate that process.

Thankfully, the Lord loves spending time with us, so taking even small steps towards him, can make a big difference. Bear in mind that you don't have to follow all of the 8 steps at once. If your life is anything like mine, you may feel right now that you don't have time for any of them.

Start small. Challenge yourself to make space for one of the suggestions, just for today. Then try it for another day. Once you feel confident with that step, try another.

You need to be intentional about this. It's about forming new habits. Experts say that it takes at least 21 days to form new habits and more recent research suggests that it can take as long as 6 weeks. So don't be too hard on yourself or beat yourself up about it, just make a decision to stick with it and you'll soon reap the rewards.

Disclaimer

Sadly, I can't <u>guarantee</u> that you will hear God's voice. Ultimately, that's between you and the Lord. However, by taking the steps outlined in this book, I believe you will be putting yourself in the best position to make that connection. It worked for me, so my hope is that it will work for you too!

Part 1

Grappling With God

Learning to hear God's voice and knowing his will.

"...plans to prosper you and not to harm you,
plans to give you a hope and a future."

- Jeremiah 29:11

The Troubles Of Life

A few years back, I had been drifting along in life. I had been on track, or so I thought, slowly building my confidence in hearing God's voice.

I was happy enough: I was enjoying my marriage, I had a steady job, I was involved in church life and dabbled in different hobbies. We had one child and a little girl was on the way.

Then the unthinkable happened.

My daughter was born with serious health issues and required immediate emergency surgery. This led me and my family into an extended time of hospital visits and extreme stress. Then, as we were still recovering from all of that, the news came that I would be made redundant. Already at rock bottom, it felt like I was being kicked while I was still down. I couldn't see what the Lord was doing and I felt as if I was spiritually deaf.

The Lord intervened by prompting me to go on a course called "Tools For Freedom". Through that, he transformed my life. I realised that I was more worried and upset about my job, than I was about my daughter! My priorities were all wrong and so was my thinking. He revealed to me that there were spiritual strongholds in my life and led me through the process of demolishing them.

The details of what happened on that course is another story, but part of how I walked out my new-found freedom was learning how to listen to God, all over again. In the process, I found new ways of making space for God in my busy life, ways that I will share with you here.

Becoming a Christian is an exciting adventure. At least, that's how it starts out.

If you're like most Christians, when you first discovered that there is a God, that he is real and that you could know Him intimately, it sparked a revolution in your life. Your desires changed from being self-centred to being God-centred.

You found out the Bible promises that God has a plan for you, "plans to prosper you, and not to harm you, plans to give you a hope and a future" (Jeremiah 29:11). Then eagerly, you began to seek God in prayer for that plan - for you and for your loved ones. You didn't want to miss any of the good things He had in store for you.

Perhaps your life has always felt like that and you're just as excited today as you were when you first met the Lord. If so, then that's great! However, the reality for some Christians may be quite different.

Barriers To Hearing God

If you have a prophetic gift, you have another reason for wanting to hear God's voice. Hearing from the Lord is the foundation of prophecy and is the first step, when you pray for others. You want to be sure you are hearing clearly, because you want to bless other people with love, dignity and integrity.

For many of us, we learn to love the sound of the Lord's voice, but we hear it in short bursts, like snatches of conversation. We long to find the time to hear Him more clearly and more often, but somehow it feels like life gets in the way.

All kinds of issues can contribute. Maybe:

- In the daily routine of work and busy meeting schedules, you've lost touch with your goals for the future.
- The effort of getting the kids up, out of the door and on their way to school has worn you down and is sapping your desire to pray.
- You're stuck in a job you hate, or with a boss you don't get on with and you can't see a way out.
- You're dealing with a bereavement or some other trauma in your family and the flood of emotions drowns out the voice of the Lord.

If you're struggling to pray for your own situations, you may not be praying for others either. One way or another, your prayer life and your gifting begins to take a back seat. Eventually, you find yourself giving up and accepting second best for your life. The problem with busy lives, is that we can end up running on auto-pilot, doing things because it's expected of us, not because it fits with God's plans and purposes.

We may think we are taking control of our lives, but as we drift from one crisis to another, we can find the very opposite is happening. We begin to lose control of events and emotions …and spend less and less time hearing God's voice. Eventually, we become frustrated and may begin to wonder if God is there at all.

When we do manage to find time to listen to God, other barriers may get in the way:

- Sin blocks access to the Holy Spirit and needs to be confessed in order to hear God clearly
- Pride can make us feel that we don't need God's input and prevent us from seeking him from our hearts
- Bitterness about our situation can make us blind to the truth about God or ourselves and leads to self-deception

Together, these barriers can result in four issues, each of which impacts on the next:

1. Fear: The frustration of not hearing God's voice, leads to a fear that we *can't* hear His voice. This fear begins to block up our spiritual ears and makes it harder to hear the next time we try.
2. Uncertainty: When we do hear something, we become unsure of whether it is God's voice, our own voice, or that of the enemy.
3. Doubt: When we start to question God, ourselves, our motives and our abilities, we may lose confidence in our understanding of God's will for our lives and project that to other people. Prophetically, this can lead to poor delivery when we try to share what we hear with others. We may even clam up completely and never share anything.
4. Paralysis: We become so afraid of making mistakes that we become paralysed, unable to decide what to do next. This leads to further frustration and the whole cycle starts again.

Good News

However, I have good news for you: God wants the very best for you and his heart is for you to be free.

I found that by taking a few practical steps, I was able to enter into a deeper relationship with God than I ever thought possible.

My desire is that you'll be able to do the same, begin to break out of the old patterns and get back into a loving relationship with your father God. As you let go of any false sense of control in your life and listen to him, you'll be empowered to know him better and work in co-operation with Him once more.

We'll look at those steps shortly, but I want to start by laying an important foundation for you.

While I recovered from the issues surrounding my redundancy, the Lord brought me back to something that had been important to my faith since I first believed in Jesus: the need to *experience* God and spend time in his presence.

Right from the start of my Christian life, there's always been something deep down in my spiritual DNA that knew I needed to be close to God, to meet with him personally, every day. And this is what he has brought me back to, at every period of my life.

I've often felt like Moses, when he was told to go and speak to Pharaoh on behalf of his people. He knew that unless the Lord went with him, it would all be for nothing.

I realised this same truth: that if I don't actually meet with God, if I just go through the motions of religion without the reality of an ongoing encounter with him, then I am wasting my time and potential. If I don't encounter God every day, then I am unlikely to hear his voice!

As a result, my passion is to encounter God as often as possible and lead others to do the same. Our need for that encounter is the subject of the next chapter.

An Encounter With The Lord

Jacob had an encounter with God, which earned him a new name. In Genesis 32:24–31 (New International Version), we read the following:

So Jacob was left alone, and a man wrestled with him till daybreak. When the man saw that he could not overpower him, he touched the socket of Jacob's hip so that his hip was wrenched as he wrestled with the man. Then the man said, "Let me go, for it is daybreak."

But Jacob replied, "I will not let you go unless you bless me."

The man asked him, "What is your name?"

"Jacob," he answered.

Then the man said, "Your name will no longer be Jacob, but Israel, because you have struggled with God and with humans and have overcome."

Jacob said, "Please tell me your name."

But he replied, "Why do you ask my name?" Then he blessed him there.

So Jacob called the place Peniel, saying, "It is because I saw God face to face, and yet my life was spared."

The sun rose above him as he passed Peniel, and he was limping because of his hip.

The name Jacob means "he grasps the heel" or "he cheats, supplants",[1] which turns out to be a good description of his younger self. Prior to his divine encounter, Jacob was a grasping man. He was used to getting what he wanted, even deceiving his father in order to obtain an inheritance.

However, when he met the Lord on that momentous night, he wrestled with Him until daybreak. Jacob wouldn't let go until he received a blessing. He got his blessing and was given the name "Israel", which means "struggles with God" or "strives with God".[2] But he was also marked for life, with a limp.

Being marked with a limp may seem strange to us, but it was a very real part of God's blessing. It was a permanent reminder that God was in control of Jacob/Israel's destiny. From that point on, the Lord worked in Jacob's life to change him and bring his disposition into line with God's purposes and character.

The biblical record tells us that in his final days, Israel asked Joseph to bury him with his ancestors. When Joseph agreed, Israel "worshipped [the Lord] as he leaned on the top of his staff" (Genesis 47:31). Later, when Joseph brought his two sons to Israel for his blessing, Israel recognised God's sovereign choice that the younger son would be greater than the older. Israel had changed to serve God rather than himself.

An encounter with God brings about transformation. That was true for Jacob and it's also true for us. If we want to hear God's voice, we need to encounter him regularly, in order to grow and deepen our relationship with him.

"An encounter with God brings about transformation"

[1] Holman Illustrated Bible Dictionary, p860.

[2] Harper's Bible Dictionary, p434.

A Lifestyle Of Listening

Our encounter with the Lord may not be quite so dramatic as that of Jacob, but his life teaches us some important lessons. Hearing God's voice isn't a one-off experience, it's an ongoing relationship, one we need to grapple with. This is a lifestyle of listening.

As we listen to and wrestle with God, He will leave His mark on our lives. We are already made in the image of God, but there is a further deposit of glory that he wants to place in us. For believers, this is the promised Holy Spirit.

As we are filled with his Holy Spirit, we are changed. God fills us with the character of Christ, transforming our hearts and minds - and enabling us to hear His voice more clearly. Scripture calls this "the weight of glory" (2 Corinthians 4:17).

How we establish and maintain a lifestyle of listening is the subject of the rest of this book.

Part 2

Hearing God

"The Lord came and stood there, calling as at the other times, "Samuel! Samuel!"
Then Samuel said, "Speak, for your servant is listening.""

- 1 Samuel 3:10

1. Find Time to Be Alone With God

Throughout the rest of this book, I'm going to encourage you to listen to God primarily through prayer, which is really a one-to-one conversation. I'll explain that later, but first I want to tackle the one thing you may feel you don't have: *time*.

The Trouble With Quiet Times

Learning to spend time with God is the first step in creating a lifestyle of listening. It's something I learnt early on in my Christian life. However, I have concerns with the way traditional quiet times are sometimes taught in church.

I don't know about you, but the phrase "quiet time" conjures up visions in my mind of moments where:

- I have to sit down with my bible
- I have to talk with God
- I have to do that in a prescribed way and order

It's inflexible and presents two problems to me:

1. The fact I *have* to do it can make it a chore, rather than a joy.
2. I can end up limiting my relationship with God to those few minutes of official bible reading and prayer.

However, I think this stereotype surrounding the quiet time concept means we end up missing the point. It's not about times and places and formulas. The Lord is bigger than that. As I said earlier, it's about relationship.

God is the most loving and amazing being in the universe, so it's easy to linger in his presence. He wants nothing better than to spend time with you and he doesn't mind if you don't pray or read your bible, particularly when you're worn out.

Despite what I have said above, there is certainly a place for discipline in the Christian life. Read your Bible when you can and pray as often as you are able, the Lord will love that. If you already have an established time when you are alone with God, then so much the better.

What I want to encourage you to do, is to find times, *any times*, when you can be alone with Him. This might be a quiet time, first thing in the morning or last thing at night. It could also be at any other time of the day. Make space for Him, whenever and wherever you can, *throughout* your day.

The reality is that if we're serious about getting close to God again, then we have to spend time with Him. It's the same with any relationship. If we want to get to know people, we have to find time for them. If I want to grow and cultivate my marriage, I have to make time for my wife.

> *"If we're serious about getting close to God, then we have to spend time with Him"*

I have spent many years commuting to work, by car. My journey is usually between 30 minutes and an hour. These occasions are some of the best prayer sessions I have ever had. I don't really enjoy the journey itself or being stuck in traffic, but I miss those times when I go on holiday with my family, because I don't have the same opportunities to just "be" with my Lord. I have to get creative.

Here are some possibilities to help you find time during the day:

- Maybe you commute, but you're stuck on a train, with a lot of other people. Plug some headphones into your phone and listen to a bible talk. Or pretend to listen, but close your eyes and pray.
- Maybe you're in a very fast paced job and can't seem to find any time outside of that focus. Try using a toilet/rest break to take a moment, even if it's just 5 seconds, to acknowledge God and ask Him into your day.
- Getting the kids to school? Plan to leave the house earlier (they're

probably awake anyway) and bring a few books they can read in the car, while you pray. Or read bible stories to them.

- In between lessons at school or college, try getting to the next class a little early, so you have a minute or two to ask the Lord to join you there.
- Seek God while you're doing chores around the house. Use the times when you're doing tasks involving relatively little brain work, to pray and praise your Lord. Washing up, ironing, painting and decorating are all examples where you can do this.
- Set regular alarms or tasks on your smartphone to remind you to turn your thoughts towards the Lord at various times of the day.
- Start a prayer journal and make a note of each time you acknowledge God's presence during the day. Check it at the end of the week to see how you did.

These are just ideas, so ask the Lord for inspiration for your situation. Keep doing these things and soon enough, it becomes a habit. This is important because as we cultivate the habit of spending time with God, we provide more opportunities, more often, for Him to speak and for us to listen.

2. Find the right place for God

Sometimes, you need physical space to be alone with God. This is about finding places that take you away from other people, so you can have your encounter with the Lord. Those other people could be your spouse, your friends and colleagues, or your kids.

Please understand that I'm not talking about going on retreat for three months, without your husband or wife. What I do mean, is to find places and environments where you find it easy to be in God's presence and hear his voice.

If you're stuck at a desk all day, then it may not be conducive to hearing God's voice. Find an excuse to get out of the office and into a green area, like a park or some woodland. If you're surrounded by people, then find a quiet place you know people don't frequent (though bear in mind your personal safety too, especially in the dark winter months).

If you're stuck at a desk all day, then it may not be conducive to hearing God's voice.

I have a park I can go to near where I work. Every day, I make a point of getting out of the office and walking there in my lunch break. If it's a nice day, I'll find an empty bench to sit on. If it's cold or rainy then I'll take a slow, winding route through, in order to maximise my time with the Lord.

The park comes with the added bonus of exchanging the drabness of the office for natural distractions like birds and trees that help give me perspective on my day. I've lost track of the times when the solution to a problem at work has presented itself to me, whilst I have been on one of these walks.

The space you choose doesn't have to be anything complicated. It could be the car, as I mentioned above. It could also be:

- A meeting room at work
- Working from home and using the first few minutes to pray with a cup of coffee, before you start

- A chapel at your workplace (many schools, universities or hospitals have one)
- Your bedroom or another room, while your baby is asleep
- Finding something to occupy your kids for a few minutes, while you go into the next room

Think of one of the places you could use and make a point of getting yourself into that space. Go there today, put it in your diary, add a repeating reminder on your phone, whatever it takes to get you there.

3. Start With Worship

A good way to begin prayer, including time to hear God, is to start with worship.

By worship, I don't necessarily mean singing songs. You may not be in a place where you feel comfortable singing out loud. However, what the best worship songs do is to *point us to God and remind us of who he is*.

In the same way, you want to start your time reminding yourself of who God is. Think about his character and make a conscious choice to take your spiritual eyes off yourself and onto him. With that approach, you can put aside the troubles of the day and gain perspective on them, as you come to pray and listen. When you worship, you also create a culture and an atmosphere around you that is open to hearing what the Lord has to say.

If you're alone in the house or car, then you may feel able to worship in song, or sing along to your favourite worship track. Otherwise, you can find other ways to worship. This might be in prayer, reading your Bible or meditating on it. Speak it out loud, whenever possible.

> *"Pray or worship out loud, because there is power in the spoken word."*

There is power in the spoken word and it connects with your spirit better than when it is just in your head. And that is what we are trying to do: make a connection with God and place ourselves in right relationship with him. Even if you don't hear anything specific, you will set yourself up for a positive experience.

Remember, worship is all about God, not about you or me. It's easier to pray and hear the Lord from a position of understanding God's character, than when we are looking at ourselves or our difficulties.

You can praise and thank God for:

• His greatness and majesty
• His holiness

- That there is no one like Him
- His love for you
- His Father heart towards you
- His provision for you
- The good things He is already doing in your life

Don't be afraid to use someone else's prayer, if you're feeling stuck. The "Lord's prayer" should really be called the Disciples' prayer and is an excellent model to use. It covers everything we might need for the day, starting in worship ("our Father"), asking for His presence to change the world around us ("your kingdom come") and asking for our physical and spiritual needs to be met.

4. Pray And Ask

Jesus said, "Ask and you will receive, knock and the door will be opened to you" (Matthew 7:7) and he said it in relation to prayer. We can ask for the physical things we need, but we can also ask God to speak and to enable us to hear his voice. We all know how to ask God for things. Or do we?

Here's some common misconceptions that can get in the way:

- We may feel unworthy to receive anything from God and therefore don't ask at all
- We may have low expectations of God and ask only for little things that seem less important
- We may not understand that God is interested in every area of our lives, so only ask for the big, or important things

However, the bible says that God has made us worthy through the blood of Jesus, shed for us on the cross: he has "…qualified you to share in the inheritance of his holy people in the kingdom of light" (Colossians 1:10).

"You have an inheritance in the kingdom of God, so ask, seek and knock about everything"

When Jesus died, he took our sins from us and exchanged them for all the good things God has for us in heaven. He gave us an inheritance as his sons and daughters. An inheritance that is available to us now!

We are made into his sons and daughters, not by any goodness or good works we have, but by our faith in Jesus' sacrifice for us. As a son or daughter, your inheritance places you in the kingdom of God and the Lord wants to be intimately involved with you.

And part of your inheritance is made quite clear by Jesus himself: ask, seek, knock. In Matthew's gospel (Mat 7:7-8), we hear:

"Ask and it will be given to you; seek and you will find; knock and the door will be opened to you. For everyone who asks receives; the one who seeks finds; and to the one who knocks, the door will be opened".

God wants you to hear his voice, he wants to have a conversation. So ask him to speak to you and ask him to open your ears to hear.

Keep asking until you hear him, then ask him for more! Ask him to give you wisdom, understanding and revelation as you learn to interpret the things he says to you.

5. Write It Down

Many people with prophetic gifts love speaking out what they hear, but don't really like writing it down. I confess I'm one of those people, but I have learned that writing things down can help me to understand and confirm what God is saying.

I have therefore trained myself to write down words from God as soon as I can - I use the Evernote app for the purpose, as it is always with me on my phone or on my computer at home or work. Whether you use electronic means or paper and pen, I want to encourage you to do the same.

Writing down God's words can teach us to be specific as we learn to hear the Lord more clearly. I have used the following technique when leading small groups and found it also works well when you are on your own.

"Writing down God's words can teach us to be specific as we learn to hear the Lord more clearly."

The best way to learn is by doing, so book some time with the Lord and try it out:

1. Start off in worship and prayer, just as we have been describing so far.
2. Then, with a blank sheet of paper and a pen, start writing down whatever thoughts come into your head. This could be random words, phrases, or even simple pictures and doodles.
3. As you write, keep praying and ask the Lord to reveal the key things he wants to draw your attention to. You may find it helpful to keep pausing and review or meditate on what you have written so far.
4. Highlight, underline or otherwise mark the key words and phrases on your page and ask God to explain more about them.
5. Keep writing things down, and start looking for patterns. Similar kinds of words might point towards a theme that the Lord is showing you.

Eventually, a bigger picture may emerge from your scribbles, it could look a bit like a mind map. You can continue to pray into this, or if the meaning is clear, ask the Lord what he wants you to do about it. For example, he may want you to share a few words with someone else.

Place a date on your page and this could also be the beginning of a prayer diary, which you can review later.

I make regular space in my schedule to go back through these words, thoughts and impressions. It's incredibly encouraging to follow the different threads and see how they have changed over time. It can also remind me at crucial moments of what the Lord has placed on my heart.

6. Do Something Creative

If you don't feel you're creative, then think again. God is creative and he has passed it on to his children. We were all designed to be creative, just in different ways.

My drawing skills are somewhat lacking, but I am a very visual thinker. This means that while I may not want to draw a picture, I might create an outline or a flow chart, to help me understand what God is saying.

You could: - Draw, scribble or paint - Write a poem - Make a diagram or mind map on paper or computer - Take notes in a prayer journal - Physically express what the Lord said by your posture or position, or in dance

"God is creative and he has passed it on to his children."

One of the most powerful words I ever had for my church came to me in a dream. In the dream, I saw Jesus crucified and he was surrounded by the most amazing rainbow colours. At the moment of his death, I saw a shockwave come out from him, which echoed out through all creation.

There was a lot more to it and I couldn't find the words to fully explain the picture, so I asked a prophetic artist in the congregation to paint what I saw. We then used the painting to share the dream with the church. A picture speaks a thousand words!

If you have an artistic gift, then ask the Lord to use that to speak to you and to other people. He can anoint your natural ability to give it a supranatural dimension and a prophetic edge.

7. Make Prayer And Listening A Conversation

Remember that on the one hand, the Lord isn't just a sounding board for your troubles and on the other, he doesn't expect you to sit and listen in a vacuum. He wants to have a conversation with you.

When I was a young Christian, I was still learning my way around the idea of listening to God. I thought that when I prayed, if I caught God's attention then he might deign to visit me with a *big pronouncement* of some kind. I would then be able to share it with everyone (whether they wanted to hear it or not), with a flourish of "thus sayeth the Lord".

Thankfully, I have learnt that God is greater than that. He loves me and wants the best for me. He also wants the best for the people who might be caught in the cross-fire of my words for them, whether they know the Lord or not.

"God wants to have a conversation with you."

This means he also wants me to get it right, both in what I say and in how and when I say it. I can spend time with him, just for the sake of being in his presence and that's a good thing. If he speaks to me, that's good too and we can discuss it together.

It's the same for you. If the Lord gives you a word or a picture you don't understand, ask him to reveal the truth to you. Look at the details in the picture and ask him to expand on what you see.

Seek the interpretation. Ask what the word means and how it applies to the person or situation you are praying about. Write it down to gain clarity.

Ask how to share what you hear. A word may be personal to you or the Lord may just want you to pray. If unsure, ask someone you trust to help.

8. Mix It Up

My final tip for you is don't get stuck in a rut of meeting God in the same places, in the same way, all of the time.

Some people are creatures of routine and that very routine helps them to hear more clearly from the Lord. If that describes you, then that's great: try to find ways of sticking with it.

However, many of us are refreshed by seeing and hearing new inputs, especially from our surroundings. Always praying in the same way or with the same order can eventually make those sessions stale and make it difficult to truly encounter God and hear Him.

"Stretch your prophetic muscles by moving out of your comfort zone."

If you're always going to the same place, try somewhere different for a change. I have a little game I play where I start walking and I ask the Lord where he wants me to go, as I move forward. This starts off as a simple and fun exercise in learning to hear the Lord in more detail, but can lead to all sorts of interesting times. Sometimes, I have ended up in significant conversations with unexpected people.

Experiment with different ways of addressing God with your voice, or with your posture: standing, sitting or bowing before him. You can also stretch your prophetic muscles by moving out of your comfort zone. If you're not used to speaking out loud, try speaking positive words such as bible verses over your friends and family, while you are alone. Maybe like me, you wouldn't normally draw - try asking for a gift in that area.

You don't have to do these things on every occasion, just enough to keep your times with God fresh.

Putting It All Together

I hope you have found this book useful. The 8 practical steps above are not exhaustive, but should point you in the right direction and help spark new ideas about how you can hear God's voice better.

The Lord can speak to us at any moment, not just when we devote time and space to him. However, by learning the discipline of a lifestyle of listening, we can attune to his voice, so it becomes easier to hear him outside of dedicated prayer and worship.

"Now is the time to ask the Lord for more."

Above all, ask the Lord for a *real encounter* with him, through the presence of his Holy Spirit. It is the Holy Spirit living in us who brings God's presence into our lives and who leads us and trains us in all things. We therefore need to be filled with Holy Spirit continually, in order to grow in character and in our ability to hear our Father's voice. This is not a one-off experience, but an ongoing relationship available to us every day.

If you've never been filled with the Holy Spirit before or only experienced His presence infrequently, then now is the time to ask the Lord for more. Don't put it off, or wait until tomorrow, because you'll either forget or life's troubles will get in the way.

God is speaking to his people all the time. All we have to do is listen. That means God is speaking to **you** right now too. All you have to do is listen…

I pray that you will meet with God, that you will know him and be known by him. May you encounter him every day and hear his voice clearly. Amen.

Before you go...

Now that you've finished this book, your journey doesn't have to end here.

If you'd like to know more about hearing God and learning to prophesy, then visit my website timbaderonline.com where you'll find relevant articles and a community of like-minded believers.

The best place to start is to copy and paste this link into your browser:

https://timbaderonline.com/prophecy/learn-how-to-prophesy-definitive-guide/

If you're not already a subscriber, you can join my email list (it's free) using the forms you'll see on the above page.

When you subscribe I'll send you updates and new articles straight to your inbox (on average every week or two) and from time to time, special offers and freebies, like this eBook. You can unsubscribe at any time.

Blessings,

Tim

About The Author

Tim Bader is a blogger, author, church leader and speaker.
He has worked with the National Health Service in the UK for over 30 years.

In his spare time, he is part of the leadership team of his local church and writes and maintains two websites.

He pens articles on technology and ergonomics at ergonomictollbox.com and helps people learn how to hear God's voice and apply the prophetic gifts in Christian ministry on timbaderonline.com

He also runs online courses, including the Ergonomic Toolbox and 4 Steps Prophecy School.

He lives in Surrey, with his wife, children and Playstation.

26791657R00023

Printed in Poland
by Amazon Fulfillment
Poland Sp. z o.o., Wrocław